Lairs

Lairs

Judy Brown

Seren is the book imprint of
Poetry Wales Press Ltd.
Suite 6, 4 Derwen Road, Bridgend, Wales, CF31 1LH
www.serenbooks.com
facebook.com/SerenBooks
twitter@SerenBooks

The right of Judy Brown to be identified as
the author of this work has been asserted in accordance
with the Copyright, Designs and Patents Act, 1988.

ISBN: 978-1-78172-666-2
Ebook: 978-1-78172-667-9

A CIP record for this title is available from the British Library.

The publisher acknowledges the financial assistance of the Books Council of Wales.

Cover artwork: Roger Mattos, from @linearcollages

Printed in Bembo by Pulsioprint, France

Contents

| Lairs & Cages |

| Curtilage |

| Apertures |

| Lairs & Cages |

Postmonkey

As the ship speeds up at Pluto, the earthlight sensors blow.
Lights fade to pastel touches on your toffee-coloured fur.

The flight recorder picks up your first words three years in:
a garble of Merriam-Webster, harsh against the hum.

It's not long before a halo'd planet sets off some chimpy whinge
about a green place and your females smoking red in spring.

When you give up hope, the language programme hits its stride:
more dopamine, more titbits, an electrode's neat incentive.

In the slow lane, a terrace of dying suns, you learn to really talk.
This one is your lab tech's voice; you're asking about stars.

Decades in the leatherette pod the psychs designed for you
turn your muzzle silver, and the low-grav wrecks your bones.

Your tail must be bald as a bike-chain, the way you grumble.
I transcribed your words on landing, the part with the needle,

where you're yelling you're not ready, won't be rushed.
The cargo hold opens and you're wiped, then flushed.

Settings

That was the day I discovered the tick
in the place a navel piercing would sit.
It was just a dot and I scratched it off with a nail.
I'd been in Scottish rooms for days
reading John Cheever's thready journals
underlining the bits where he expresses self-hate.
On the internet they were vile and interesting,
hard-bodies with a corona of grippy legs.
The sated ones swelled to shiny cabochons,
mottled as frogs, in sockets of queasy skin.
A lot happened later: the tick was irrelevant
like jewellery you wore in a dream and lost.
I never had that one, just the usual teeth
rattling into my palms like a jackpot.
The omens bore no fruit. The tick had no precursor.
We swam through half-term, keeping no records.
Even though I had scraped it off and soaped
the place, somewhere it bloomed, underground
like an iron-rich gem, awaiting its wearer.
Scotland was famous for its perfect raspberries
and a kind of stone named after some mountains,
the colour of ginger ale, in an ugly brooch.

Fish. Oh. Fish

'Even snakes lie together' – D.H. Lawrence ('Fish')

Your egg eye is open and you look worried.
    You're the scaly junior lawyer at midnight
        falling short on her target of a year's billable hours.

Corporate fish, you're bright as pain, sliced up.
    You share the water with a spill of inky stripes.
    Your kind blaze colours fine as banknotes.

Oh, fish, you have whisked up a clever curve
    defining the future as it draws itself into a fist.
    Then the evening comes on, pistachio and blue.

You breathe and flex between bars of dark.
    A clerk could still walk into the hot, open night
        leaving a jacket on the back of her office chair.

A lit anglepoise floats above the papery desk.
    There's a deep anglerfish clocking the hours.
        No one must turn off your light while you are gone

or there'll be nothing to swim back to
    but a scrunchie of kelp, uncounted on dry sand.
    Little fish, everything that matters happens here.

Fruit for Offices

In long glasshouses we bloom inside our skins
on plants obedient to the fertiliser piped to their roots.
The fruit must swell with dispensed water
but never to splitting point since we are for display.

The company provides bowls the client is free to keep.
We share nothing with the windfalls the staff bring from home.
Our curves are as contrapuntal as a composition,
of small amendments made at the nutrient's origin.

We are carnivals of eugenics: picked over, intentional.
No one hungers to milk our tidy molecules for sugar
to flout god. Few of us will know what it is like
to be bitten, how hot and bruising a mouth can be.

No one risks being driven out of anywhere,
head-down and cringing, by the conference organisers.
As the meeting circles us, the taken minutes rope us in.
We are the daughters of the oligarch:
golden, wooden, whom no one wants to touch.

Cravings for Pure Sugar

Out of nowhere in the dank kitchen
came the need to eat rhubarb jam
off a blunt spoon. Sugar, sugar–
like thirst, like asking to be touched.
Slugs unscrewed themselves out of the overflow
and left their silver notes on the brown carpet.
The days were full of invented habits,
roasting sprouts with garlic, carrots with oregano.
Nothing drew me but the gas burner's blue-yellow coronet
and the murmurs of people who we pretended
were hardly dead. Their books shuddered
under my bitten nails, and the hype was true:
their buried voices rose from the high-end collected works
far realer than the actual mouths that came.
The poet's friend would watch the flames and make notes
while I crouched cold-kneed on the lino
spooning fructose from a hexagonal jar.
Outside the diluted mountains were almost tasteless
and the pitch of the sweetness climbed
and climbed. Soon the pain from their family bereavements
hung in the air like fish cooked earlier in the week.
I kept on as best I could, the cold shrinking my skin,
and, every so often, the bestial feast of a fatless mouthful
took the place of drunkenness, of freedom, of a soul.

The Coelacanth

White half-moons of condensation rise
on the windows, water fine as sand,
until the day warms and wipes them.

Under his habits – the shower, grainy coffee,
a silk tie left coiled in the drawer at work –
beats the payload of yesterday's whisky

pressing on the day the way a bad dream
boils out of sleep. It's not the sour tongue,
nor the shiver in his bruised hand,

but some bigger dog. A call's coming:
both from his fatty, mismanaged liver
and from over the border, a place his buffed

colleagues tell him can't be. Fox stink lies
above the frost like something magnificent.
He remembers what his cashmere coat cost

and that what he saw of himself in the wink
of the smashed bottle was not temporary.
His forehead streams as he long-hauls the stairs

up to the platform. Played-out muscle swells
under his shirt's pure cotton. The concrete
below his shoe soles gives him the answer:

Jesus was called the fish. Christ, he was dry.
In Brockwell Park the Lido is open; he dives
deep as he can, down to where he can swallow.

Room Service Menu

The number for Reception is always the easiest to dial.
Open the leatherette folder and thumb
the list of what's possible; it feels almost warm.

In this chill room it's the nearest thing to skin.
Ask no question you'd not refuse to answer.
What you request will come, but less than you wanted.

All day you travelled to meetings on the city's ring roads,
air-conned in a limousine's twilit intimacy.
You played penitent, interrogator, witness, scribe.

Here is headed paper for your latest confession.
Your sole archive is one wheeled suitcase,
your available transformations: (perhaps) girl.

Now you're entitled to wipe yourself on fresh cloth.
Your traces will be incinerated, as in hospital.
Press zero, and name the liquid that will cure you.

Vivarium

'*Gaussian processes [...] allow us to make predictions about our data by incorporating prior knowledge [...] − Gaussian distributions are widely used to model the real world.*'
(https://distill.pub/2019/visual-exploration-gaussian-processes/)

'*Adding more data points causes the fitted function to adapt itself to the shape of the true function, and uncertainty decreases.*' − A. O'Hagan ('Bayesian analysis of computer code outputs: A tutorial')

The place comes in a kit like a shelf company.
The usual mean runs through the dimensions:
maybe a perch for some exotic bird.
Is the atmosphere even breathable?
At the moment it smells of nothing.

I needed to make the space homely.
I set the dials, kept the light levels low,
fed in the best guess like a pacemaker wire.
For now the prior falls like a dust sheet
over other possibilities. You can overthink this.

But there have to be rules,
or you get too far away from everything you've ever known.
It's all hearsay, what kind of beast this box will house
though we've planned for weird local behaviour
in the clutter of the higher dimensions.

You could be a snake, pretending to sleep
cool reptilian sleep along the given line.
We bide our time, hoping you're smooth −
spikes or fur, and the whole zoo might have to be chucked.

It's infinite in here, so I can only see a little way
through the smoked glass
to the pitifully few bits of spoor.
I might have made too many assumptions.
You flinch and shapeshift with what's not ruled out.

After a week I can smell the rankness in the run-off
but you're still bubble-wrapped –
a mystery parcel bulging between bits of tape.
Little balloon animal, only at the joints do you crystallise
into pivot, articulation, arthritis.

Are you breathing, or is that just thin air, huffing
at a piercable skin of what's possible?
When you made your move I was watching.
I hadn't predicted the damage to the endless corners
or the all-heaven-breaks-loose uncertainty deflating
then falling from your bones,
              like dandruff, or scattered light.

Small Visible Queen

From across the Channel she is all I can see.
Her outfit is silk with a pattern of Greek keys
interlocking in yellow and black.

Her people, she imagines,
must be grey and tender, rising like dough
and, oh so easily, knocked back.

Her elected ministers hardly register
though their bellies dome like stadiums of flesh
with veins in a blue you can't see but which makes you uneasy.

The newspapers from this morning
are already ripped to tassels and rippling in rain.
The sooty sugar has been licked off the buns.

She commands the sea and the clouds
to do what the Meteorological Office predicted.
It's only manners to make people feel safe.

She has heartburn, a heat rash and might be
hypertensive, she is neat and turned like a bobbin.
She twirls and pretends to patrol.

When she sleeps, she's as hieratic as a chesspiece.
Teeth and hair are the things people notice.
Her teams drill and coil through the Buckingham night.

The Larder

In the shop's moist basement the red wines lay
prone in their cool dormitory. Beyond
the jars of lobster bisque and canned truffle sauce,
both Lancashires sat squat on their wood: *Tasty*
and *Mild* like a pair of underground kings.
No satisfaction in breaching the waxed cloth,
breaking the stiff robes they were buried in.
Only the owner had the right to draw the cutting wire
twice through the horizontal before quartering.
It was ritual, to bear each portion upstairs to the shop.
Later we'd peel the cloth off the soft edge
and unpuzzle the grain of the clotted blank face.
Down there, too, was where they kept the unripe moons
which were soft as what's inside a baby's unfused skull.
In the dark they would salt to rock and start to spin.
When at last the old satellite has worn to a nub,
an uncut cheese will rise, white and purposeful
with the sun's reflected buttermilk light, to do its work.
Think of the store of teeth a shark is born with;
which, one by one, drift to the front of the mouth
to take their turn to be the ones to shine, to bite.

The Royal Forests

In the royal forests, the chimera was idling
by a mirror pool, calm as a self-driving car.
In the royal forests, my breath moved slowly
against the pile of my blue velvet snood.

Lichen was lime green and frilly, as it clasped
the oaks' new growth. The scar of a cut branch
would burst in spring into a brown firework.
It was all starting again, the dynasties, the cooking:

game, and jugging and spatchcocking
in the quasi-taverns skeletoned in gold wood.
Light pooled in certain places, and from others
it kept away, like indigo around a wax resist.

I hurt my hand in the royal forests:
a splinter got wedged down behind my nail.
For a long time I didn't realise, about the birdlime
and the stage set, and the twinkling.

I didn't realise that the investment,
and the visiting henchmen were incidental,
that it was about the bark, and the water
ascending the tubes in the trunks' rinds,

that it was about the trees, not the haunted air
that peopled the gaps between them.

Greenery

When I moved to the city that no longer exists
it was September. The air was brown fur
growing thick round the candy cane buildings
that poked through cloud and were lost. I could
breathe, I could talk, but my bones grew longer
and rang when sheet lightning flashed its show
over the mainland. I ate without using knives
or forks – not to be feral, but to slow myself down.
Under the fridge lived one single cockroach
I saw when I ran to the kitchen at midnight for ice.
It was mannerly, seemed not to breed. It knew me.
But I lost myself in the mirrors that covered
one wall of the lounge. I wanted to multiply,
fatten into a crowd. When alone I spoke
of myself as 'we'. The local clothes suited
me well, and I bought my own air conditioners
to plug the square holes that pierced the walls
of each bedroom. In the evenings I drank and murmured
in the first-person plural, the trees on the hillside
across from the block cooed back from the mirror.
I could hardly see my green self through the trunks.

Working From Home

I was sitting in a room with five windows.
A picture window to the meadow
Spread heat across my back.
The glass implied a pentagram
Of which I was the midpoint, facing a wall.

The room's central axis
Ran down my spine like a long plait.
A big mirror with a glass frame
Threw back a sixth window in my face.
It lent my skin a citrus glow.

The press of nothing
Was forcing open my well-kept mouth.
I was a green man necking ivy.
I was a green woman piling up
Gallons of lime air in my oesophagus.

The time of day was open.
The mirror meadow was more real
Than the real field could hope to be
With its soft coat of grasses
Uplifting their buoyant seeds,

With the small white dogs and their owners,
With the day that was coming.
All of these ingredients I would use in a ritual
As if this would not, in another era
Have cost at least my life.

The Visiting Princess Tries to Snip a Tiny Rose

Her tin eyes glittered while the panel beaters
gonged gorgeously like a national orchestra playing at home.

Her winter nails were like sliced good teeth, refusing any light
that was not bleached. The hothouses had been a beguilement,

but now she was sweating. Shark-tooth thorns glared at her,
newly-waxed and disarmed. She had some advantages:

her hair, coiled around her ears in a traditional hairstyle
as labour-intensive as handmade shoes; her pumiced hands

whose narrowness she fluttered and mentioned; her dress,
which stood up without her in it because she was never in it.

Until today the rosebaby had blossomed and snuggled in its garden cradle.
It had never seen a blood-fleshed human break and enter

its omnipotent unfurling story. When it learnt to speak, within seconds,
wolfish and fluent, the russet foxes and squirrels, who had never

travelled far, bristled their red fluff, surprised at what a shrew it was.

Another Young Man Chooses Water

Colleagues report he drank bottled water
for the white-knuckle ride of works drinks,
as they wobbled on their bar-stools.

Organic chemistry unfolding in their guts,
they didn't notice much.
Like, when did he leave by the back exit

to stand, exhilarated
at the river's familiar honking checkpoint?
To touch the thick, soaked wood

of the boat piers might have
steadied him. What happened next,
our investigator hopes to discover.

Fluxville

The sea turned over quietly
at low tide, scratching its flesh.
Seaweed was piled up
like old clothes baled for export.
The estuary water made sense
of what it means to find your level
despite the land climbing up and over
and sinking down in parts
like something undisciplined.
I was not rich in patience
but I waited because moving forward
to greet the future is something
I feel a woman shouldn't do.
I turned my back on the tide tables
and slept in my day clothes.
Soon enough it was high water:
the harbour brimming, the water silky
with the queasy half-set wobble
of a substance almost on the turn.

| Curtilage |

Sea-Want

There is no menu so I order a steep glass wall full of eroded sky
fusing subtly along a horizontal axis

with sea of a dull, base metal sort, grey as lead
and, with white caps at its tips, like lead exposed to vinegar.

I can feel its leady weight, even on the finest days.
Its pools are like a litter of lead pigs joined to the swish sky.

This sky itself has cohesion, like a pale blue cheese,
or a tearable curtain rotted by sunlight

but it's holding firm against the dark swallow of the universe
that hangs behind, waiting for us to squander

our handhold, toehold, finger-grip on rich loam, our legacy bioblanket
and parachute silk sky. Here we're miles inland in fact.

We only imagine the view-light entering the window over the marina,
the tomato juice sunset like a coppery respray of our property dreams,

while the sky is chasing its soft tail far away at the coast
in a cup from the pale and seamless kitchen, from which we do not drink.

Towards Gentrification

When you walked with me along the Thames
the sky was an arch of purple dirt.
Under our feet: cement and discarded aggregates
and, for a little while, the greasy boardwalk
        of the city wetland reserve.

In the past there were so many moths, you said.
Metal was clanging on metal behind us and below
the holy city across the water, which was lit
to be immense and imaginary. In my memory
        you had no smell.

This time our mouths were full of cement.
You had a better watch and shoes than before
and they tethered you to the place you belong now.
But even these filaments loosened
        as the night fell
        into plum and charcoal.

In parts the past was glued to the present
but we walked separately through mineral dust.
Across the river they had untied the cranes
which swung in unison like a choir, upriver
        and away from us.

The river clenched and spilled
between the Thames Barrier's silver cups.
Nothing was freed and, in the distance,
        whole new cities glared with light.

The Property Market

From Platform 1, Blackfriars Station

There's something over-familiar about the cranes
rising through the city. For centuries its huddle
was spiked only by the paraphernalia of spires.
Through the river-soaked glass of the new station
we can measure the torturer's bamboo as it grows
into a friable body. The shallow-rooted boroughs
might be peeled off, easy as a roll of turf.
Here the earth has already crumpled, spills skeletons
which are coppery-blue from buried money.
Skyscapes are a story I'm bored being bored with.
Still, the latest towers are eating light like plants,
donating grace as they hurry into their final poise.
A confession has been exacted, then simplified.
All that remains as we sink down into the tunnel
between platforms is the city's current heraldry,
its long bones opening our skulls to the air.

&ℭ

The Islander

By lean August, you're sure that scent is a myth,
not the island's honey skiffing over the strait
as fragrant as some attar of all your what-ifs.
Then the girl in the skirt sewn from headscarves,
her face lovely and sun-ruined, pipes up
spinning the bar staff a confection of lies
about bees as big as boiled eggs, and lilies
which turn their trumpets to follow your trek
across sky-baked uplands of angelhair turf.
Her eyes have that look, iffy and mazed
by something no man can charm into mineral fact.
Don't get her onto the purse-sized leverets
who lift soft muzzles to hiss your deathdate.
Stand her a Malbec before she fuses the lights,
or the Gulf Stream swerves inland at her call.
Whitebait straighten, re-silver, swim off your plate.

ဆာလ

The Reunion

While I had become sanctimonious and fat
your lounge had an appealing double aspect.
You seemed to have no books, several kids.
Outside the sky was an octopus expanding
over lumpy trees, a sketch of the Barbican.
I think you asked me something, but in code.
There were biscuits, unctuous with white chocolate
and chopped apricots. I held onto the advice
I might have given you. You would
after all, treasure my phrasing for decades.
My skin was travelling in the wrong direction.
An observer would say you warmed to your theme.
It wasn't hard. The balcony was spiked
with rosemary and sage, a single white chair.
If you tried to touch me, I certainly shook you off.
I wanted everything you had. I had to leave.

৪০৪

On Not Leaving the House All Day

The leather sofa never unsaddled me
from dawn to this late dusk.
I cowered under my books' verticalities
and watched the windowsill make its shadow play
on the closed yellow curtains.
In the lit world, the scaffolders married
each shackle and pole with a screamy bolting.
Everything I was used to doing seemed wrong.
It's not grief, I am not that kind of claimant.
Underneath my skin I was writing a message to you:
not so much a howl as a business plan.
I'd already sent it long ago in triplicate
from a newer body than this slumped shape
waxing the sofa with her unbathed sebum.
I'm still ordering cone wool off the internet.
It comes greased. We unwind together.

߀ߣ

The Property Market

I took the interactive tour,
spun on my axis in a Highgate lounge
while the ceiling mouldings swam away and up
in little waves of vinyl matte peristalsis.
I was astral projection, my body soft
but in a less toothsome way than meat.
The agent and I twirled, hands flung out,
round the kitchen that only appeared trapezoid.
What about the locked door, I asked.
They told me, *shh, you can climb onto the flat roof*
but it's not mentioned in the lease. The owner
is out there now, oiled and peeling,
having forgotten it's almost not his home.
It was bad for him, not just the dodgy easement
but the constant interruptions, including me
swimming round the master bedroom with a fish-eye.
He came back wrapped in a red towel,
said he wouldn't sell if I was the last girl on earth.

৪৩

Waiting for the Pomegranate Boat

(in response to Muriel Spark's novel 'Robinson')

I strung my noticing eyes on a rosary,
and clicked and confided.

On the island I stuck to the facts;
they were slippery and touchable as blood.

The crater's lava groaned and sighed
folding itself over itself, like laborious student soup.

The goat died, the cat lived;
the moon had a pulling power I'd never felt at home.

Three gashes, like fish gills, in an old jacket
were a red herring, but I never forgave their extravagance.

The blood was feint, the lurid mustard field
food only for the eyes.

The blue-green lake had me under surveillance
so I folded my hands in my frosty lap.

I practised being inside the others' faces,
code-switching my mouth to let them speak.

I kept my eyes peeled. I lived like sea-glass,
hard, clean and opaque.

Sounds grated mildly on my ears.
Most days I was disinclined to be kind.

North of Here, South of Here

The weather shoulders in from the south
baking the foot-thick front of the house
or it comes as rain, like someone splashing in a bath.

What's most of it but some thirst in a vector?
The bottle shop's open and you might as well.
Pompom bees bump at the windows and bad luck

brings them through the vent too often,
to be found like beech mast, light and brittle,
on the upstairs windowsill where the paint peels.

I blew from the south, butting in,
certain I could join the circle chanting at the fire.
What people want is the same everywhere.

When storms come the temperature drops fast.
The other world falls under a sea-bird cliff.
Transport links fail like a burst necklace.

Some days only the sinkhole makes sense.
The yard faces north, the vicar's ivy swelling
over the wall that's as high as the cottage.

Nothing comes from that direction;
but as Autumn grows its belly
that's the route the light takes to leave.

The DIY Forums

a woman games the August bank heat
earning the usual dry hands in a run of DIY
rolls putty across her palms to soak up
touch as rebate wood draws linseed oil
from the glazier's smooth beige dough
she wants to say as it becomes soft and warm
think of babies! the matte the way it plugs
gaps almost a stopping of tiny soft limbs
pliable as cookies she runs a plumbline
widdershins whilst behindhand with her nails
all different lengths despite the emery board's
insistence on the perfect almond shape
her veined hands now opening the canister
great for toughening rotten wood on the site
they're debating drying time how long till
the putty puts on a skin of human cells
and are both types of paint OK water-based and oil
the men on the forum mostly say no
in the Q&A but she still plays the hand
she's been given as a creature cooked up
from mixed fats plus a crushing majority of water
while her windows' bodies are singing themselves dry
may not last the red winter one man says
in a short season could lose their honey

The Frog Prince

This man believes a woman can feel the muscle
of money changing his skin, a second landscape
mapped over pectorals, biceps, his long back.

It's a language that means she reads his body
in several translations: rare metals unfold
in the altered curve as thigh flares into buttock.

It's not about the palm's pleasure but signification.
No woman loves him without moistening her lips,
the word *price* commingling with mint on her breath.

She keeps his heat and spill in her throat: *investment*.
This is exegesis, the note of the glassware, the snap
in the lift to the thirtieth floor. The actual moment

is nothing, it's about what she learns of her value.
Down on the cushiony carpet is a private education.
You cannot touch me, he says but she's expected to try.

Under his eyelids the message is: amethyst bruises,
unpettable dogs, as his hands mete out a currency
that more than repays the damage done to him.

The Unfair Coin

There is a face on it.
I turn the coin in my hand:
the same face mirrored on the obverse.
It runs through the metal
like a pipe of quartz worming through rock,
a cavity filled with its own stubborn light.

She is an offering to herself,
not a token I have the right
to toss and gamble on,
her face a single face on both sides,
a tube of face the coin was sliced from.
Inside, the double walls of her teeth will never part.

The Queen's eye in her face is a tunnel of eye
stretching as far as it needs to.
Within the coin, her inner ears
listen to each other, part of the same ear,
the same tin can linked
to itself across a bedroom
with a taut string.

Between them is no new information.
Nothing but bad luck lies
between the double strike of the press.
You could die in there,
the Queen's unending rope of a face
streaming through your body like sound.

The Fourth Wall

All the while you sheltered at home in two rooms,
these estate agent's streets were laid out, lilacs
fumbling over brown brick walls like cartoon gelato.

Walk, and here it was, bettering the park:
the masked vegetable delivery man in his shorts
shouting have a good day with the boxed produce.

You were even able to see inside the open door
the stairs facing and, to the side, a lounge
white and with a low shelf unit along one wall,

a sense of backlight suggesting French windows,
a garden. No sign of the person who took the box.
Now our nosiness goes unrewarded, the desire

to step inside is sour enough to sting. You wouldn't
tell everyone you don't much miss being touched.
The extended trees across from the blue garages

are all moving differently, like a bouquet of vegetables
or other girls with the same hair colour as you
so it's easier for people to rank you. The pulses

beat in their recycled storage jars like an investment,
or the whole huge contents of what you've done,
the pilot light of your body's reputable wants

only recently turned down at the ovaries.
Time hit you at the right moment perhaps,
so you can lie in bed like you used to

before you were able to get anything
but when you'd just begun to want it
in a way that was humble, and also a bit like despair.

| Apertures |

Ways to Describe Motion

We'd been drinking and trying to talk about maths:
a question I had but didn't know enough to frame,

and next morning my back locked like a finished Sudoku
and the doe was nibbling at bullet apples under the tree.

All I could think of was the preposterous geometry
in her efficient body, and its surprising depth at the tail

like a tall trapezium turned on its side; so angular, not
an obvious sculpture of muscle like a horse's rump.

It was shocking how narrow some parts of her were,
her neat muzzle barely the size of a toy dog's nose.

I kept thinking, a child could have held it shut.
She was listening with the joke petals of her ears,

sometimes for minutes, then she'd carry on strolling
and nipping at the growing points of shrubs.

When the moment came, and she – what?
began to move off, like something coming on stream,

her tiptoe legs were altered: I saw how much
speed she had in them, and how much information

about how to move could be wrung out of her,
and them, when you understood the techniques.

Judas's Rule of Three

With the first smile I try
to reach into each of the punter's eyes
and to place myself, staked,
mid-pupil, like Leonardo's
man, spatchcocked.

I remember not to really look
lest I get drawn in, the hook
that catches their windblown
hopes can turn and nick the fisherman,
the maggots' squirm becomes delicious.

The second smile is the feint.
You make it look half-hearted, not meant.
You lean and draw. Because you love
his robe, his silky beard, his mouth,
pulling back is hardly possible.

And again, you catch his pique.
He's honest but, as any saviour, he's needy.
He'll wonder when you cooled
to lukewarm and you'll see the holes
hammered in his big eyes widen.

It's not that he thinks he's lost
you but he's counting what you might cost
him. With your third smile comes ease,
and you clap his thin shoulders
like a politician. The shadowed watchers

suck air through the gaps in mis-
matched teeth, start to close
as his answering smile rises
like a blaze. You love him. He
loves you. It's never free.

Three Chinese Boats You've Never Seen

It was you the harbour's scum winked at
from the intolerable gap that swells and narrows
between a junk and the steps at Blake's Pier.

Out in the Lamma Channel, another girl's feet skidded
off the white plastic roof of the junk. She fell:
horizontal, so far overboard her head hit nothing

but water as her wine glass spiralled empty.
You were never one for swimming, then or now:
the sharper pleasures are prone to puncture.

We know you loved best the ferry's first morning run
to any one of the outlying islands. Upstairs
the glassed-in aircon slapped the others awake

but on the muggy lower deck men gulped
noodles from red bowls in a fog of engine noise,
as a spam treat floated pinkly on every soup.

So many near-deaths by liquid, you grew coy.
Let's turn instead to the photos of us just dancing
on the slippery bar, or play back the water's

fidgeting after the engine died and all the boyfriends
except yours, pissed over the side of the sampan.

Some Security Questions

Q: *What were the stupid questions?* A: There are none
the statisticians said, but this was maths, so they could
be out there, capable of being asked. You might find one
holed up in some hard-to-fathom 5-D keysafe
downwind of the site manager's office. Q: *Are any cats kind?*

A: Some questions crack your teeth on the way out.
Harmful as polonium, they pose a risk even to the poisoner.
Experts say you can handle them, like dangerous dogs,
by whispering your mother's maiden name
into a magnetically constructed containment device.

Q: *Your first school?* A: Asking a question doesn't rid you of it.
You still own the dog, pouchy and violent. OK, the agent
would text you the code in Health & Safety's usual 2-D.
But when you reached your hand into the opening
your mind couldn't seem to accept what came out.

Our kitten was pretty shaken up by its first mirror.
At this age you've anthologised all your worst shames.
The others are safe as plasma in the toroidal machine.
Q: All I ask is an evening viewing my second-best humiliations
in B&W, the old dog back on the sofa. It's the best question
and I deserve an answer. A: *It happened, and this is what it was like.*

The Landlady

There were those too poor to roll candles,
Who ran a thread of rag round a saucer
Of the last fat rendered from an animal
   Whose every bloody part was used.

Like any eye in a room's corner
A bullseye burned, breathing off his smoke
Which like all that comes from the body unprocessed
   Gets called dirty.

Still the cloth gave a nifty light to our home,
Warm and watchable. When mentioned
Such lights are said to stink but then why not
   Keep silent?

I chose a bear, whose body fat is gold to them.
They own it under their loose furs
While they cool all winter and their minds
   Sky-vault out to other lives.

We met, by chance, and out of our bodies
So now, you see I live alone.
Put down your duffel, roll the dice or flex the cards.
   Trouble me for your fortune.

In the corner the bear's eye boils in his dance of fat.
   We have not abandoned the gods yet.

Charcoal

You come upon the stack, sealed with cool earth,
smouldering for a work week in a clearing.
The shack nearby is for the man who tends the fire.
In the old stories a loner has his uses,
and the charcoal burner uncovers what is hidden:
the red king with the red throat, the local girl's
mossy camisole and the two plastic tumblers.
He reads the words no one wanted broadcast
so they painted them over with grease and soot.
He speaks as he finds because all that matters burns,
or is drawn from the woods on an open barrow.

Something good must happen to the wood
in its slow tent as oxygen is greened out
and ash buds grow pistachio-black and eloquent.
After a week, its bones are sweet as balsa.
The stories never say who wanted the charcoal.
It might beat white in a copper barbecue
under fish caught so young a curl of fennel covers them.
Some of it ends here: feathering itself over paper
finding out the four corners of the life model's
lanky cricketer's body, carbon singing carbon,
fire blurting every consecrated thing it knows.

The Three Gods of the Heart

The mimic heart will learn to sit in a surgeon's hand,
ectoplasm in the form of a phone. It's fast as rats.
It tots up the risk in every alternative future – burn or leave.
The real heart sleeps a ragged sleep like a dog by a fire.

It's the father we were told to love, slow with heavy maths.
Once in a while we find the funding to make him lift
his occult platinum gaze and churn his thoughts
across one careful question, like an eclipse traversing.

The cost is huge. The birds stop singing.
He takes half a week in the transect, every light squibs.
Here and now the gobshite son is flush with information
distributing it all over the shop, plus or minus his cut.

On the table is the offering, a tenuous box of blood.
In its panic mess, you can hardly distinguish chamber
from valve, unplait the lumpy piping. It's nothing but spirit
from which the surgeon is burning away the scars.

The heart's electricity will test it like a halo, or wings.
The nimble son of man is near at hand, the absent father
saying little in a supercooled warehouse. Wish us luck.

The Data

The assurances we sought were malleable as plasticine.
　　No one said: *not everything can be smooth.*
Not every song segues into another enough like it
　　to keep dancing: the disco transitions into sour light
with couples pulling back from a littered floor.
　　The assumptions we were making deprived our eyes
of the freedom to see the break in the ice,
　　the phase transition from satisfactory to all fucked-up.
Let's hear it for code burned into your liver by a rogue surgeon:
　　it's a claim, as in a time capsule: *things were like this, once.*
You can read from the graph that sometime later
　　another kind of thing seemed to be going on.
Behind us lay the environment where the process could be visualised
　　with a fitted curve, an undulating graphene sheet, consistent data points.
In front: the cliff and the new information
　　from which we at last deduced what is happening to us now.

The Hero's First Telling

The hills acquired a terrible roundness
from the faint grey shading on their northern slopes.

What I saw in the far distance
I gave more credence than the spreading blood.

Make no mistake, this was a tableau
whose lurid choreography I'd be destined to re-enact

in future gestures as inappropriate as memes
when hailing a taxi or checking the lockedness of a door.

We were both altered: he was freed from his skin
while mine was put under tension because this was so new

which made me revere his current spoiled simplicity
and be glad I wasn't the one lying in the sand.

I was dressed for harsh weather and began to sweat
as my hair and beard became grizzled with dust.

You're hearing it before it becomes legend;
I just shivered and found my teeth too big for my mouth.

But I did go back and change into fresh linen
and order pink and green cocktails at the hotel bar

where I saw you looking over, and smiled,
though you were closer in age to the man I'd killed,

where you'll come to share my table when I beckon
as he would have, had he been the one to live.

Brink

I voted in the rain, and the edge seemed firm
but rounded so as not to cut your fingers.
The usual women with their tick-list of names
gave up their time to sit at the folding table.
I believed in it all, the thick perfume of the trees round the estate,
the community centre's spacious lino,
all its other tables folded away, the privacy of the booth.
I voted and I hesitated. I could smell the edge here
cutting the air the way the sea's movement smacks it into ozone.

The edge was sucking up everything before the counting,
the air peeled and rolled down into a thin sheet,
like stripping off a label. I looked, thought
I could see something I wanted, then the polls closed their mouths.
Finally, the edge was a single paper cut moving
inside my clothes as I changed the position of my arms.
By morning there was no edge, just a sharp olive-green plain
where I stood on the margins of the open ground
not yet understanding. There was no other air than this.

The summer when the rest of the world seemed to be burning but it was only the start

the campus was spliced in whole at that point
rain spun through its dog-loop over and over
whilst a gamut of magpie and rabbit let us
spend our last puppy-time on alps of caretaken turf

always men gutting tunnels through laurel
baby-handling huge trees right from cast seed
then the short art film, the incision sealed over
straight into sideburn autumn, satchel lids flapping

clipped to who-we-were lanyards by inbound hands
the eye blinking and turning down its lumen lastingly
the bodies' return to their own time improbable
opportunity for the gull colony to come down hard

on the loosely-held chicken roll at a picnic table
the future inhaled the hot months like an old hoover
no lit-up chink in the current black rubber tube,
hands paper-dry, the animals thinning out, and us

spraying human speech from fur-lined lips
the light of a flick planet on-and-offing till gone
unhomely among ourselves the dry blade takes its turn
de-pilling our skin-fabric to one furious itch

On the Front

The woodlouse crawling down the sea-wall
was transparent, almost precious,
a decent grey, warm like the wool of herdwicks.
I wanted all the neutrals; I wanted you
as you were years before, thin and miserable,
casting yarrow stalks onto lino for hidden reasons.
Grey / untouchable, I wrote in my diary.
I wrote a lot about that one time you almost touched me
when you helped me unlock the door of the flat.

There's colour on you now: your tan leather shoes
and you're drawn to the city's younger nightspots
though always reflexive, ready to be evicted.
I think you couldn't afford to have a body then
though now I notice your skin is quite gold
and your jumper is petrol blue. I'm still looking
for the neutral state of those stony walks:
your grim colourlessness; my lurid want
balanced and still against something implacable,
some grey concern for me, some cemented misfortune
you had selected and applied to yourself.

Steeped

We are swimming through strong brown.
All light has turned to tea, a mild infusion.
Warm grey curls off the paintwork.
Our actual ankles are ankle-deep in soft shadow.

The windows are curtains of dry rain
which drop like dirty waterfalls from their frames.
Each object is outlined with a cushion of shadow.
The mothers-to-be are swollen with babies

made of shadow: they don't allow talking.
They spit moths of dust into their teacups.
Oak trees are bouncing on trampolines of shadow.
Even outside, the same rules apply.

The mothers-to-be pat their must-filled bumps.
The floor is a skin of lion-light and mink-shade.
When the test proved positive, the dentists poured
the mercury from their teeth and stopped them with shadow.

I am the barren girl off to one side.
My chest is so flat, it captures no shadow.
The unstoppable grey falls on me nonetheless.
I delight in the fireworks of my monthly bleed.

While it lasts the neighbourhood dogs cannot settle
in their beds of straw and serge,
and the pigeon-grey landladies bang on the pipes
in case something gaudy could be flowing.

My Latest Era

Bring it on, I said, fizzy with rhetoric.
Then the dark trees struck up their electrofunk.
I was passed this parcel inside which everything stopped.
When I unfurled the layers, it was full of oil
which fastened down the sea's exciting waves.
The babies I might have had coughed in it like gluey seagulls.
My skin, no longer impossibly balanced between bloom and die,
became as useful as if it was man-made.
I was becoming permanent:
that other possibility that can happen to flesh
if it isn't shocked out of its bloody self early on.
Artists track the new vectors of my facial skin.
Graphite hisses in the life room like rain falling.
Be happy, I said.
It is doing what it wants to now.

The Baby Tooth

The first hug for months came from left field,
undefended. I didn't invite it but couldn't not accept
its probably-safe investment in the press of two bodies.
It left me punctured, outflanked. On our walk,
my sanitising, after touching stiles and gates, sagged.
It seemed I'd saved all my touches to spend
in a single evening's lush spree. Once I'd shifted
into reverse, when the friend we visited laid out
three separate packs of Walkers Crisps, one each,
I fed from them all, spreading my risk like the rich.
I bought wine in the Co-op, held it, stroked it, strode
into her house as if into a hospital, unwashed as a landlord
whose money was only a peril to other soft touches.
I cut the cheese, patted the bread, smeared
myself on the evening like a dog in a garden.
I accepted the hug on leaving because in for a penny
with my dark haptic practices. Even my own house I defiled:
flossing and removing my lenses without ritual cleansing.
In the night I touched (for luck?) the last baby tooth in my mouth
then sucked that finger, sacked everything precious. It tasted
ash-bitter, evil with sanitiser I'd never washed off.

A Model Life

'The **birth–death process** (or **birth-and-death process**) is a special case of continuous-time Markov process where the state transitions are of only two types: "**births**", which increase the state variable by one and "**deaths**", which decrease the state by one. The model's name comes from a common application, the use of such models to represent the current size of a population where the transitions are literal births and deaths. Birth-death processes have many applications in demography, queuing theory, performance engineering, epidemiology, biology and other areas.' (Wikipedia).

I'm waiting for an occurrence having the character of an arrival
In that it flowers irregularly into some sort of expectation
The floor suddenly notices its high polish
There is no appointment system, but I imagine anxiety
Sometimes it can be a paper letter, delivered by bike courier
As I sit in a state, shivering, in some videogame lounge
Or you are trying to raise the call centre, in the thick of it
And yet nothing really changes as you move up the queue
When you tell me you didn't know how you got there, it creeps me out
I bring out the old envelopes self-consciously
They are parchment, dusty pink, from Conqueror Bond
And so contaminated the price sticker has turned grey
As the ink flows, I can't shift the sense of quietness
It's as if no one else wants to be involved
The system is steady, the fungus-infected fish flapping to keep afloat
The tank has the dark blue beauty of a snow globe
Outside, a street party slaloms between growth and decline
People become drunker, or more sober, by the usual increments
While my fingers work a crochet hook in and out of baby clothes
When the news comes – *surprise!* – it's in an email
From your regiment, to say there's been an accident with your horse

Birthday

The day opens like eyes open
spreading their willingness generously
across the desk's polyurethane varnish
like butter right to the corners of a cut brown loaf,
ordinary but brand new and hot,
bought cheeping in a white paper bag.

The day opens like beaks do
to show the long pterodactyl tongues of birds
in a painting of hell. But everyday birds
also have these sorts of tongue, so it's fine.
Their throats synthesise honeycomb noises
like ingredients piled in a blender goblet,
so very ready to be smooth.

The day opens like hands,
mine dry from the dull work
of disinfection, to make sure they are holy
before I touch my mother's cup.
When I meet the mirror, my whole skin
closes up again, like a jumper felted in the wash.

The day opens like a parcel,
and I have two, untouched for 48 hours.
People are shedding more, with the new variant.
The third parcel came today, a small rip
flowers to show gift wrap inside the brown.
I won't be opening it for a while.

My Comeback

I came back in style in a banker's back seat.
I came the back way behind shutters of darkness,
under the click of raindrops as big as earrings.
When I returned my back teeth had loosened.
I threw up at every service station en route.

Beyond the flowered screen a squat table lamp wicked
and glowed. My Northern accent slunk back.
Several auto-immune reverses ran on red alert.
This was me, towed along in the backwash
squirming inside a borrowed blue cagoule.

I wasn't talking: it wasn't worth it.
Instead I watched the burgundy tree.
Its trunk was every kind of darkness. As always
I had the best room. The answer came:
'Don't ask questions, they hold you back.'

At the back of a fridge the element gathers fur
and my face began to itch as soon as I arrived.
Unease hung in the air like the minutes
that follow a dog-fox. I counted comeuppances
and dabbed my boots with Neats Foot Oil.

I'd like to say I returned retuned, my lock-jawed clock
kicked into reverse. I wanted to whisper: *'I'm back'*
like some brawler in an action movie.
It's as beautiful as it always was. No cures then,
but I got the bastard thing off my back.

The Victory Parade

The dazzling chevrons on my hide say nothing
of the kind of horse you'll find beneath the skin.
Zookeepers are wise to fear our chisel teeth
and it was for a joke that I persuaded all the tribes
to kill their flocks and trust the clanking bony dead
to rise up, split the ground and set them free.
Alive, I trot, insouciant, through loops of bunting
the minister's supporters strung between the posts.
The devil's here – in his usual circus outfit.
I let *Him* ride me: he's the only one who can.
Today I am respectful, full of stagey mirth,
as I lift and point my polished hooves.
Even before we knew, clowns were on the turn.
All through the previous stinking summer
Nick's cocked ear had been retuning the ground.
In the distance, two stripy tents, like nipples
topped with tassels, fly the winner's standard.
The sky is turquoise. Jesus, what a shade!
My hooves are tapping, obedient with felony.
Some new concoction boiled over today.

Our Acts as Dreams

Awake, I miss the syrup comfort and lush 1-D
of a good dream's generic moments.

Ask the emergent creature (me), cresting up with a yawn
from the hand-painted waves (bright and bog-standard,

lacking in bite but with good camera angles) of sleep.
We are all novices at this, becoming ourselves daily

out of a solvent liquid. It's an opportunity:
I place myself delicately in water as you would

an individually-priced gerbera, topping up
the stale vase to a finely-spiced shimmery boil.

Each dawn a new animal climbs out washed
and a little peeled, having shed nothing permanent

but yesterday's longlisted bric-a-brac and a few
whisked-up anxieties storyboarded into surround-sound

yet always somehow painless. Again, come up for air
to the alarm tone you picked from an extensive menu

of chimes, spouting prophecy like a pure vessel
until the world pulls at you with its specific fingers

drawing out the thread-veins of acted habit. The day is sunny
so, of course, for a minute this morning seems new.

Steam Tables

Steam Tables and Properties of Steam: Useful Tables for Engineers
(Babcock & Wilcox, 1936)

The kitchen table creaks, to show the dead are close;
oiled pine smoking like dry ice, there is so much to tell.

The gauge of our lives will build in increments.
Here they are laid out with less faff than a horoscope.

The book is tiny, a squat landscape, covered in red linen,
the paper hardly ginger. I read the contents to you over breakfast.

It belonged to your friend's wife; he knew you'd enjoy
the old titles lifting like wet air above a simmering dye-pot.

It's not just to please you that I study the columns
of steam's exploits. Measurement swims between us

while water is just liquid, pondering its possible costumes.
Even a size up I pride myself on retaining a female ratio.

Hardness of water depends on the speed of a stranger's car.
Absolute viscosity of fluids, and the areas of squares,

sides advancing by eighths. Soon they were courting.
How long before the tide sleeved the ankles of the jetty?

My fingers click, the future wonders whether to flood or trickle.
The present worth of an annuity? Nothing yet. Later will be hotter,

steamier. I want so much for us to live. She could read
the patterns in these tables as she could her own knitting:

snowball earth, sauna; sky split with whited-out water.

winter a dropped stitch

people were saying fuck January is stretching out
this year but I love its cool panthery length
had been too snug for half a decade
small and cold against my HRT-altered body
chilly in the gap where the dressing gown overlaps
a v-neck full of openness to the things to come
while the humming of the communal heating system
made for a sticky pasture under the Crittall window
a snow bomb forecast chaos across the country
but the city cooks from inside so we felt no shame
judiciously weighing the loose parts of our bodies
like a stakeholder's medium-sized store of grain
felt pleasure for the first time this year, uncompressed
vital to take walks, collect vitamins from the sun
and store them under a papery skin by arranging
the shaken body under cold light on a balcony
everything slackens honey drips from a spoon
sharp heart expanded like a smile breaks a face mask
it was nippy but I generate a compost-heap warmth

Acknowledgements

Some of the poems in this book appeared first in the following publications and places - I'm grateful to their editors:

Ambit, Arts & Culture Exeter University website (www.artsandcultureexeter. co.uk), *Coast to Coast to Coast, Finished Creatures*, www.johnfogginpoetry. com, *Magma, The Moth, Mslexia, The North, Perverse, PN Review, Poetry, Poetry Wales*, 'Project Boast' (ed Rachael Bentham & Alyson Hallett, Triarchy Press, 2018), *The Scores, The Scottish Review of Books*, 'SPARK: Poetry and Art Inspired by the Novels of Muriel Spark' (ed Rob Mackenzie & Louise Peterkin, Blue Diode Press, 2018), 'The Tree Line: Poems for Woods, Forests and People' (ed Michael McKimm, Worple Press, 2017), 'Truths' (ed Sarah Barnsley & Peter Kenny, Telltale Press, 2018)

'The Islander', 'On Not Leaving the House All Day', 'Steeped' and 'The Coelacanth' were runners-up in the 2018 and 2017 *Mslexia*, 2017 *PN Review* and 2015 Resurgence Eco-Poetry poetry competitions respectively. 'The Baby Tooth' won third prize in the 2022 Ware Open Poetry Competition.

Particular appreciation goes to Barbara Marsh for many hours of invaluable skype thoughtfulness, and to Kathryn Simmonds for her subtle noticings. Cheers to Angela Cleland, Ed Barker, Ed Reiss, Katrina Naomi and John Stammers & the Group for commenting on individual poems. The usual love to my good friends and family.

Thanks to Hawthornden Castle for a wonderful month's Hawthornden Fellowship in spring 2017.

I'm also very grateful to Arts & Culture Exeter University and Exeter University's Institute of Data Science and Artificial Intelligence for an Arts & Culture Fellowship in summer 2019. This allowed me to collaborate with Professor Peter Challenor and his team of mathematicians specialising in uncertainty quantification, giving rise to a number of the poems here. Many thanks to Peter, Dr Danny Williamson, Dr Hossein Mohammadi, Dr James Salter, Louise Kimpton, Evan Baker, Victoria Volodina, Dr Jen Creaser and Professor Beth Wingate for their patience, eloquence and eye-opening conversations, and to Professor Tim Kendall, Sarah Campbell, Dr Katie Finch and Jill Williams for looking out for me while I was there.

Some of the poems had their origins in a sketchbook collaboration with Derbyshire artist Wanda Brookes.

Notes

p 16 – 'Vivarium' – the second epigraph is from an article by A O'Hagan published in *Reliability Engineering and System Safety (91(2006), 1290-1300)* and available online from 10 January 2006 (download link: https://www.tonyohagan.co.uk/academic/pub.html)

p 37 – 'North of Here, South of Here' – the title owes something to Ken Smith's title 'East of here, west of here' (*Wild Root*, Bloodaxe, 1998)

p 47 – 'Three Chinese Boats You've Never Seen' – The title was triggered by a comment of Roddy Lumsden's on titles, the poem came a long time after.